My Mom and Me Together We Dance

Simply Living with Aspergers and Tourettes

My Son and I The Dances We Do

EMILY FAEHN-SHEEHAN AND PARKER FAEHN

PHOTOS BY RACHEL AND SEAN BLANFORD AND TOM RICE

iUniverse, Inc.
New York   Bloomington

My Mom and Me Together We Dance "Simply Living with Aspergers and Tourettes"
My Son and I The Dances We Do

iUniverse books may be ordered through booksellers or by contacting:

iUniverse
1663 Liberty Drive
Bloomington, IN 47403
www.iuniverse.com
1-800-Authors (1-800-288-4677)

ISBN: 978-1-4401-1519-6 (pbk)
ISBN: 978-1-4401-1520-2 (ebk)

Printed in the United States of America

iUniverse rev. date: 4/17/2009

I would like to dedicate this book to ~

My beautiful son Parker, thank you for helping in writing this book. You have grown, my son. Your fears may be a challenge for you at times but they do not paralyze you as much. Know that you can do and be whatever you want in life.

John, thank you for every time your eyes shined as you read my writing. Thank you for every "WOW" that you expressed!

To my friends and family, thank you for walking on this journey with us, and for all your understanding and kindness.

Kristi and Joy I will forever be grateful to the both of you.
Kristi you have been a big part in Parker's growth. Thanks for never giving up even in the hardest of times.
Joy, I love that you are fearless and gentle at the same time. This is truly your gift.

Miss Harriet, Thank you for touching my life as you have. Rest my friend.

Because ~
Emily

INTRODUCTION

As I thought about this book, I thought about who Parker and I are. Then I thought about all the other people out there who share in the same kind of day that I have. I wanted to let you know that you are not alone and there are many of us living the same day. The fears may be different, as well as the battle. Please know as you're in the moment, feeling whatever it is that you're feeling, you are not alone. All of you are 'Amazing' people. Maybe you are tired and truly busy people. Never the less, Amazing is who you are!

Then I thought of all of you on the outside looking in thinking, "Man this is crazy." Some days it can be crazy. As you're looking in I ask that you not judge any of us who do this every day. Love us and our child. Have compassion and maybe a hot meal every now and then. And know that it takes an exceptional amount of understanding, compassion and love to be a part of our lives to. If you have questions, please ask. I may not always have the answer but together we can find it, or at least find something that makes us laugh!

Husbands and wives love each other and know that together you are one. If you're single, there is a man or a woman who will be the perfect person for you and your child. Men and Woman, if you find that person to be special, know that their child is special too!

My beautiful you

So much you want to know

Over and over and over again you ask so many questions

Pure at heart without a thought your words come from your mouth

Sometimes they are of anger and frustration, as your thoughts race through your mind

Only you can understand what it is that you command

Some days there are fits of rage and you feel as if no one else can understand

Here you are my son; today is a fresh new day

Big smiles upon your face as you go along you way

Days have turned into months and here we are my son

Many changes in your life

Unanswered questions, fears and many tears

I hold you close in my arms as you fall asleep

Months have become years and you my son, have grown

You are standing up on your own

Your knees may be shaking and your thoughts may be racing

But you my son, my beautiful one are conquering those unknowns

You my son, my beautiful one, are my 'HERO'

I love you,

Mom (2007)

This is me, Parker. I am 10 years old, and I am in the fourth grade. I like to ride on roller-coasters, draw, paint, read and eat potato chips.

This is my mom, Emily. I won't share her age with you, she's
The Best Mom in the whole world!!!
She likes to paint, sing, cook and have our friends and family over.
She loves me, my brother and my sister.

About three years ago, a therapist told me and my mom I had something called Asperger's.

What a *Big* word.
And what did this word mean?

My mom read much about Asperger's. She talked to many doctors, and therapists to get information to help put together a team for me. All I knew was that inside of my head, it felt as if things were spinning around and I would get frustrated. I was told first that I had Tourettes; I would tic all the time. Sitting still was hard. I would get frustrated and angry. I would hit my mom, or I would throw things. I did not mean to, I just did not know what to do with the feelings that I was having inside of me. Three years have gone by; I have an awesome team that helps me and my mom. I have a skills worker, Kristi. We have been together from the beginning. She comes into our home, or we go into public places where we do skills work. I have a play therapist Joy we have been together almost a year. Both Kristi and Joy are the 'Best'!
I also have a doctor that helps with my medication, and a social worker that is always there to help me and my mom with any need that comes up.

Come along with my mom and me as we share our adventure with you. Maybe you'll see a little bit of me in who you are. For those of you who may know someone with Aspergers and/or Tourettes, or who lives with anxiety, maybe this book can open up a new understanding for you.

There are a few things about me that I have a hard time with. Words are one of them.

I do not understand terms like "when pigs fly" or when I ask a question and the answer I get is "we'll see".

Pigs cannot fly, and what will we see!?!?

When people talk with me, I need them to say what they mean.
My thinking is literal, and it can be hard for me to read your face.
I can get confused when words and actions are different. Jokes can be hard for me to get, and if someone was to play a joke on me I may get mad from the confusion I felt.

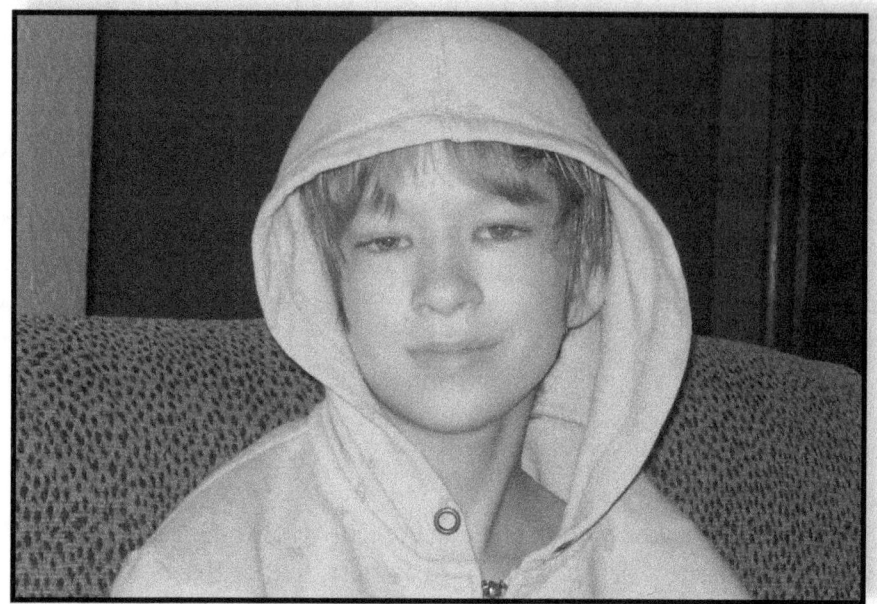

The other thing that bothers me is loud noises.

Big Booms from thunderstorms
Loud voices and loud music… these make me anxious.

In therapy, Joy taught me to use my hoodie as a tool. I always wear a hoodie if the noise is too loud. When I get overwhelmed with a large crowd, I put my hood on and focus on quiet thoughts. This helps me to be calm.

Bright lights are hard for me as well. I have many pairs of sunglasses because the sunlight hurts my eyes. When I go to the dentist, the big bright light that he uses is hard for me.

I have skills every week. My mom and my skills worker Kristi have said that I have come a long way. Sometimes it was too hard for me to go out in public. When we would go out to eat, I would spend more time under the table than sitting in the booth. Sitting still was hard. It seemed like forever to me. And if I wanted something, instead of waiting for the waiter to come to us, I would just yell across the room for what I needed.

Kristi and I started going out to different public places to practice. She taught me different skills for waiting for my turn and talking with a softer voice while we are out. Mom and I practice this as well, and I have gotten better. When I got better at sitting still, my mom took me to a fancy restaurant and we ate cheesecake!

Sometimes when there are many people, I can feel anxious. I've learned that I can put my hoodie on, or I can ask to leave. We have had to leave the movies, gatherings at our friend's homes and even Disney World. My mom is good at understanding what I need so I can do the best that I can.

Sometimes it is hard for me to use my words. I know what I want to say but it is hard to say it. I can get scared, and I fear how people will respond. Will they yell at me? Will they lecture me? Will they ignore me? Or will they listen and hear what it is I have to say?

When I am at school or with people I'm not comfortable around, I am quieter. Over the past year, I have learned how to express my feelings by drawing pictures. With Kristi's help, I started writing letters and now in therapy, where I feel safe, I started using my words. It's a hard, scary thing for me to do, but I am glad that I am learning. Sometimes my thoughts can come fast and my words come out all jumbled up. I can get frustrated, and sometimes I will growl when this happens.

When I am with people that I know, I feel safe and comfortable with them. There are times that I act up, with behaviors such as blurting out words. Sometimes they can even be a swear word. I will repeat a word over and over when I'm nervous. I often interrupt when others are talking. I will often forget my thoughts, so I will talk over others to make my point. The hardest thing for me is not to blurt out my thoughts. I do not mean any harm; sometimes I just say things. If I see someone, or something that was different or hard for me to understand, I will say my thoughts. Sometimes when I get anxious I blurt out words, I don't even know that I am doing it. My mom will ask why I said that, and I will not know what she is talking about. My mom is helping me to see that I am important, but I do not always have to be first. I can learn to wait my turn and put others before myself. I bet some of you who are reading this are thinking these behaviors sound like any ten years old! Some of my behaviors are typical of a 10 year-old; the only thing that is different is how my brain works and how I respond. My mom can explain to you in more detail about that.

The way I think and do things is different from someone my age. People call me names and make fun of me because I am different, or they can join me in my daily adventures. I love to have fun and play. I love to learn new things; it can be a little bit harder for me as I'm trying to understand. I may want to be in charge of what we are doing, and I may have a harder time processing what we are doing. Sometimes I may sit in my own space and still want others close by. Sometimes I can be overly aggressive and need reminding of other people's space. What I need the most is for people to slow down and to listen and hear what I am saying. Help me if I need help or comfort me if I need comfort. I can get scared easily. I can worry a lot. Sometimes I can get stuck on a subject forever. I can talk, talk, and talk about things that I like. Sometimes I dream about things that I obsess about, then I will talk about them some more. It's like I get a thought or a want in my head, and I can't let it go. Some of the things are good things, like learning and information.

I love to learn. I read every day. The one thing I love about my brain is when I read something, I remember it. My mom says I'm like a sponge. And yes, I did have to ask her what she meant by saying that. I look nothing like a sponge!

Sometimes I can get overly focused on things that are not good for me, like video games. It's okay to play some games. My mom is careful what I play and how long I can play. If it was up to me, I would play all day.

There are things about me that I think are awesome and fun. I think and do things with great detail. I love to draw, and my mom is teaching me how to paint with water colors. It's fun to do, and it relaxes me.

There are times that I am so uncomfortable and my heart can race fast. I just have to remind myself to stop and do what I have been taught, like taking long deep breathes or having a happy thought. I like learning how to be a better me. There are times that I can forget to do this, and I will just "lose it." I don't like when this happens. When I'm done I feel bad… My mom and other people forgive me and help me to see what happened!

Consistency is important for me. I need to know what will happen during my day. I do not like the unknown at all. I can get worried and I spend all my time thinking and talking about what is going to happen yet I have no answers. So *no* surprises please!

My mom is helpful and each night she will let me know what my tomorrow will be like. Sometimes, she will post a note as a reminder for me. If there is one thing that I can share about people with anxiety and Aspergers, it's that we are people with feelings like you. We may see the world a little bit differently, so we may need some understanding. You may have to explain to us in greater detail and you may have to say it more than once.

And please do not get offended by all my actions. In clear words please tell me what I am doing, so I have the chance to learn.

Piece of mind may be hard to find
Look within and see what is there
Take the time to give self care

Remember who you are and what it is you like to do
Be kind to yourself, hold on to your identity
Put a smile upon your face and know that you are beautiful

Piece of mind may be hard to find
Look within, can you see who you are

Beautiful…That's you!

Sheehan 2009

My son
And
I
The Dances that We Do

I call this part of the book "The Dances that We Do" because of the never-ending unknown of what our day will be like. With Aspergers and Tourettes it is a minute-by-minute change in mood.

My hope in writing this part of the book is to be able to share with you, in *simple* everyday life, what it is like to parent a child with Aspergers and Tourettes. Also, I hope it will help give a clearer picture to those who may know someone that has Aspergers and/or Tourettes yet you are unsure or may be uncomfortable around them.

If you are a parent with a child that has Aspergers and /or Tourettes, I hope you can relate to our story, and for you to know that even though your life may be a bit crazy, you're not!

Before we get started, I would like to say, whether you are married and sharing this time in your life with someone, or if you are single and doing each day alone, give yourself a *big* hug. Being a parent of a special needs child is not easy. If you are married, be kind to one another. Help one another out. Give one other self-time, and remember to hold on to each other when times are hard. *And find time to be married!*

If you are a single parent I can relate: long days at work, appointments that you can't be late for. It's all on your shoulders, maybe some of your friends or family will help when they can. Be kind to yourself. When times are quiet, relax, remember who you as a person, and give yourself time to be.

Parker was seven years old when we were told that he had Aspergers and Tourettes. When he turned three, I noticed a change in his behavior. He was obsessed with vacuums, among many other things. He became aggressive when he was frustrated and he could not sit still. By contrast, he spoke at a very young age and before he was two, he knew all his primary colors and his left from his right.

I first noticed his changes after we had moved into our new home. He loved to play yet he was shy and not as outgoing. Although there were many children in our neighborhood, he was afraid to ask someone to play. He often could not get past going halfway up a drive way before he would look back and be apprehensive to go any further. If the kids were outside, there were one or two children who he would play with, but he did not venture much past that. Having children over to our home was hard for him. At first, I thought that he needed to learn to share. After awhile, I realized it was hard for him to have friendships. He would play in the same room yet he would play separately from the other kids. He would often get upset with the children he played with and hit them. I did not understand why he was doing this, and the parents of the children were not sure if they wanted their children to play with him. He seemed to get along well with adults, older children and younger children.

As time went by he was unable to sit still. Dinner time was a zoo. Getting him to eat was hard and getting him to sit still in his chair was next to impossible. Every five p.m. seemed to become the "Witching Hour" at our home; you never knew what was going to happen.

Even before we were told about the Aspergers, I saw that Parker did better on a consistent schedule. I made his meals at the same time, I bathed him at the same time, and he had a bed time that we stuck to. He seemed to need his sleep; he would usually sleep twelve hours a night.

Taking Parker out into public was hard. His dad and I would take turns going out, or we would not go out at all. Sometimes his grandma or his aunt would baby-sit for us, so we could go out together. We often enjoyed the peace and silence that came in those moments.

I decided to take Parker to a Homeopath. After asking many questions and observing him, she was able to help us. I thought maybe we were on an uphill change. The remedy helped for a short while before he reverted to his behaviors and even more.

He became more aggressive and acting a bit odd. When someone he did not know very well came into our home, he would act up. When they would try to have a conversation with him, he would only answer using one word, usually a color. He would repeat the word over and over, laughing out of control. There would be times that he would get so worked up that he hit our guest.

He often would suck on his arm until he left marks to relieve his frustration and sometimes he would hit himself in the head. Over time, our family had shut down and we all became numb and alone. You may be asking yourself, "Why didn't they take this child to a doctor?" The answer is no insurance, and at the time, both Parker's dad and I believed in natural medicine. I did not look any further into his behaviors. I lived not knowing what would set him off. He would often hit me to the point that I would have bruises. During this difficult time, I often felt alone and I began to struggle with depression. It wore on me to watch my child each day have dramatic changes and not have any answers.

When Parker was five, his dad asked for a divorce and we separated. Parker and I left our family home and his behaviors worsened. His anxiety and fears were huge. Life was in a tail spin for us. I had to return to school so I could get a job to support us. All this, as well as a couple of moves, were not only hard on me and my other children; Parker was use to his mom being home to meet his needs. Now he was going from his home, to Grandma's, then to Dad's. He started seeing a therapist, and he shared with her as well as he could. He had so much anger and confusion. Because of the depth of his troubles, his therapist recommended us to another therapist that specialized in this area.

Meanwhile, Parker's fits became less controllable and more violent. He would lose control often, particularly in the car while I was driving. He would kick the back of my car seat and I would have to pull the car over until he stopped. At home, there were times when I would sit behind a closed bedroom door while he sat outside, angrily ranting. Although I would try to hold him and calm him, he was often inconsolable. As I sat alone crying, trying to figure out what to do for my family, he would yell and demand, calling me names like stupid and idiot. He could get so worked up over an emotion that was going on inside of him. There would be times he would get so exhausted, that he would fall asleep right in the spot that he was losing it in. I often covered him and left him there to sleep. Sometimes if he woke up, he would come into my bed and snuggle up to my back. People would say to me, "Why do you let him get away with that behavior?" I knew that this was more than *just* a behavior. There was so much that was confusing to Parker and his anxiety was very high.

Parker also had difficulty sleeping. He would lie in bed at night thinking about what had happened, what could happen, and his fears of what may be.

He simply could not sit still. Every day he would run down the hall, jump on the sofa, then over to the chair, and then to the chaise lounge. He would repeat this over and over until either I had enough or he was exhausted. He also had several tics that became more apparent.

At this point, Kristi, our skills worker, came into our lives and home. Kristi was one of the few people that Parker felt very comfortable with from the beginning. He talked openly with her about his fears and was comfortable enough to show his behaviors in front of her.

One of Parker's therapists told me that if he continued to be so out of control, that he would need to be hospitalized. The first time I did this, they looked at me like I was a crazy women with her child, both struggling with a recent divorce. They did not listen to anything I had said and I had no answers.

Parker and Kristi started working together. To this day, she comes to our home every week. His anxiety became worse as he tried to discuss what he was feeling. During one therapy session he became so frustrated that he threw a glass. At that point, Kristi made a call, and we agreed to admit him to the Children's Hospital.

Finally, after four years, we were beginning to get some answers! Although I was able to stay with him the first night, the next day we were transferred over to another Children Hospital and I had to leave him. As I left, my heart fell all the way into my shoes as they closed and locked the doors behind me. Parker's face was covered in tears. I stayed strong, for his sake, until I got out of his sight. Then, I was able to fall apart.

I have never in my life done something more difficult than that, yet I knew inside of myself it was the right thing to do. I was judged and condemned by family who did not want to see past their rose colored world. I stood strong and I prayed. I had to remove myself from other people's thoughts and opinions and concentrate on my own.

Parker was in the hospital for six days. While he was there, the doctors and staff noticed his tics. He had several from snapping in a sequence, flapping with his hands behind his head, picking his teeth and clearing his throat. They performed tests and we both had individual sessions with the therapist. During this time, Parker also went to school to keep up with his class work. At the hospital, he earned time to go to the pool and free time through positive behavior. I was able to spend an hour a day with him while he was there. The staff commented that he was well-mannered and sweet. However, only Kristi and I knew he could be good as gold in front of some people and would show his true self with others. He came home from the hospital with the possibility that he may have Tourettes. We were relieved that finally we had some answers. But a few days later, he lost it again. He slammed his head repeatedly against the wall and called himself names over and over. I picked him up, put him in the car and drove back to the hospital. He was ranting and raving out of control. The doctors admitted him again to the lock up unit at Children's. This time, I was only able to see him with an hour pass as the doctors allowed. We were then only allowed to go out in public to see how Parker would respond. They ran many tests on him this time since he showed them his behaviors.

After nine days of testing and discussions with doctors, Parker was discharged and we were referred to another therapist. She ran two days of tests on him and asked hundreds of questions. I went back the next week to read her findings. As I read what she had reported, a part of me was relieved that she saw the same out of control behaviors as well. She had noticed his inability to look you in the eyes, how he had to always be moving, as well as his tics. She commented on his need to control and to always be right as well as not being able to see things "outside of the box" so to speak, and that he had no boundaries.

Parker's world is black and white, and at the time, he was unable to color outside of the lines. She said to me that she believed he had Aspergers. I had never heard that word before. She shared with me that it was in the same spectrum as autism, but it was more the social and emotional side. She also said that he did show signs of Tourettes as well. She gave me much to read, and much to think about. I recall sitting in my car with tears streaming down my face. I was relieved, yet my head was spinning.

She shared with me about the Fraser Center, where there are skills workers and therapists that worked with children that had Aspergers. I prayed they could help us. Parker had a wonderful skills worker that was a male. Parker is drawn to females, so I was glad that he had a positive male figure in his life. He saw him once a week; it was good for him to go a little outside of the box he lived in. He had a play therapist as well. He seemed to use her more as an anger sounding board from all the hell that was going on in some of his relationships.

The divorce between Parker's dad and I became a source of fear and anxiety for him. He saw things that were difficult for him to comprehend. There were many situations in his life that caused his behaviors to run out of control. Because of who Parker is, he did not have the understanding or tools to help himself. I am so grateful for all the help that we have received. I am also grateful for all the parents that sat in the waiting room at Fraser and shared with me their days and weeks of what they dealt with as parent of a child with Aspergers. It was such a relief to know that I was not the only one, and Parker was like some of these children. I was not crazy and this was not all in my head. Names we did not share, but stories we did. There were many of you that gave me hope when I was alone. Thank you.

Using his words and confronting situations was hard for Parker. He had many nightmares and would wear my clothes to calm his daily anxieties. People would often comment on this. They did not see how this was a comfort to Parker. I was saddened and pissed by the lack of compassion and understanding of my son. It's easier to judge and make comments. "You should spank him for talking to you like that" "He's smart. Why doesn't he understand that he should not do the things that he does?" "He should not be able to act like that," or "why do you let him swear?"

Then there were those who were at the other extreme of putting Parker on a pedestal. He was perfect, and it was *me* who had the problem. There was such denial of what is a true fact: Parker's brain works differently.

As I would try to explain this to others, it became "stop making excuses for his behaviors. He's out of control." Yes, he was out of control. His life, and what he thought was safe, was now over and the anger and confusion kept building inside of him. His brain did not comprehend and there was an overload of emotions he had no clue what to do with. So, it came out in his tics, bed wetting and anger. He had more testing done that showed that at the age of seven, he was emotionally and socially at the age of three and a half years. This answered many questions, like why he blurts out what he sees or thinks. He would often blurt out if someone was "fat" or if he did not agree with you, you were an idiot or stupid. Part of this is Tourettes; part of it was he had the behaviors that a three and a half year-old would have, and when you're three, it's cute and the child is learning.

Some of it is the part of Parker's brain that says "Hey, stop and think what you're about to do or say" does not work like a "normal" brain would. So at the age of 10 having a tantrum of a four year-old. This was hard for others to understand. He was unable to do things like use a knife to cut his food; he was unable to tie his shoes. To be in a group of people that he did not know was paralyzing for him. Being in a large group of *too* many people he did know is paralyzing for him as well.

A few years ago, our neighbors were having a birthday party for their son. Parker was outside and the parents asked him if he would like to come over to the party. He so badly wanted to go. He came in and told me that he was invited and for twenty-five minutes he went back and forth. He wanted to go, yet there were so many people. The mom asked again, and I shared how this was hard for him, because of all the people. She left an open invitation to Parker. He sat in a chair and watched out the window at the party. He kept asking over and over, when will all these people leave, so I can go? We put together a gift; he sat, and sat, and sat for two hours. As people started leaving, I could hear Parker say to himself, "You can do this, Parker." Finally, only the grandparents and the cousin were left and Parker knew them all. He ran out the door so excited that he was going to the party.

He stayed for a while and was so glad that they saved him some cake. In his world, it is hard for him step out and do what he desires. He is learning, and it is getting easier, but there are still moments.

A few months ago, there was a school dance. He wanted to go, but not alone. He asked some friends of his that he has known for a while to go.

As we waited for their answer, Parker was fearful that as much as he wanted to attend the dance, he did not want to go without these friends. They were able to come, and they all had a good time. Sometimes he will need that security of what is known to him, so he can adventure out of his comfort zone.

My son is comfortable in his home, with his things. Life has to be consistent. He has to know the how and why on what is happening and will happen. In the beginning, we used many charts: charts to help him with his day, charts that told him who would be coming over in the week, as well as were he would be going. I tell him every night what he will be doing the next day. This helps him not to stay awake worrying all night about the unknown.

I had so much to learn myself; even the smallest thing like being ten minutes late picking him up caused him much stress. He would sit and watch the clock and when I arrived he would yell at me "Where Were You"!!!! He would do this with his therapist if they were running late. Parker is rigid; I had to learn to give him a time frame in case I was running late. This behavior is not a control issue for him; it is more of an unknown that can become an obsessive thought that can turn into a full blown anxiety attack. Most people can see and rationalize the situation. For people with Aspergers, they are unable to do so. This is where understanding is needed; it takes time to explain on a more detailed level, without using a whole lot of words. They do not (always) intentionally try to make life hard, or harder. I say "always" because they're human. As they get older, they learn how to play the games that some people play. At the age of ten, he is just learning how to lie, and he's not very good at it. He tells lies that a four year-old would tell and he will usually feel guilty within minutes. His first response will be "What, What" as he tries to get out of what he has done. Then, as of lately, he will quickly have humility and be honest. Lying is something that is rare for Aspergers children. They are so matter-of-fact that they can be truthful to a fault, and then they have to learn that not everything needs to be said. I'm not saying that they will never tell a lie. I see that they can do it out of "big" fear, or they have learned within their household if this is what they see.

I have noticed that for Parker, and others that have Aspergers, they can be gullible and will believe what they are told. A child at school could tell Parker a scary story, and in his mind, it is a true fact, and we will literally have to show him the "true facts" if the information given to help him understand. I have also noticed that people with Aspergers, children in particular, need to have someone telling them how to do things. This can be a double edge sword. On one hand they know it all or think that they do, but because of how their brain processes, they need to be told the basics in life as reminders and helpfulness so they can do well. I am trying to teach Parker how to think through his thoughts and to be able to do task by himself. That way, when he becomes an adult, he will not want or allow others to manipulate and control him.

There is much that happens in our day that is predictable and ridged. Bed time is at eight. There is always a battle to shower and brush teeth. Reading is until eight thirty. The same blanket, the same stuffed toy and the hall light is left on. If I ask what he would like for dinner, the answer is always chicken. As soon as he walks in the house, it is a given that he turns on the kitchen light and the dining room light, then he will walk down the hall and turn on the bathroom light, hall light and all the bedroom lights. At first I got upset because of the waste of money and electricity. As I would turn the lights off, he would turn them back on. This is a ritual that he does daily. I know when he gets in the car after school, he will need to complain about all the bad that happened in his day. I had to learn to prepare myself that he will need to vent. I also had to let him know that he has a time limit to let loose and say what he needs to say. Then he's done. I had to put a time limit on this not because I do not care to hear about his day, but with his obsessive tendency he would focus on this forever. I give him the space to let go and release his feelings, yet take some responsibility to have self control. As he has gotten older we have worked with him in skills to look at the good things as well. We practice this by starting the conversation off by sharing a good thought and not always the bad, or by asking about the other person's day, before telling about your own. Kristi has done amazing work on this with Parker. His favorite words to describe someone to use would be "stupid or idiot." This would be his response if someone did not agree with him, or how he perceived someone's looked.

Kristi decided to take him into a public setting and as a person walked in the door he would have to say a positive about them. She did this consistently for a few weeks. Now the words idiot and stupid are rare in Parker's vocabulary. He can still judge a situation and have his feelings and emotions. He almost always has an opinion, yet he has learned over the past year that just maybe others do have feelings and that your thoughts may not always be right.

My son's mood swings can be hard sometimes, for me or whoever is with him. He can be up and happy one moment and in the next, something will not go his way and all hell can break lose. Many of you right now are thinking "Spoiled child," you need to put your foot down and gain some control over him. It's not like that. Sometimes it can be a 'demanding' child, I want what I want, and I want it 'Now'. Most often he has to be first and the best, but please remember most of these children or adults are emotionally behind by years. So at 10 having a tantrum of a four year-old is not acceptable for people to see, yet in his brain this is how it works. There are so many different dynamics to Aspergers.

In some areas he is advanced and acts like an adult, in other areas he is as young as a child of four. How many of you have pre judge when you are out in public and you see a meltdown happen? In this moment things are not easy in their minds. There are no rationalities, they can be worked up in a tizzy and in that moment they are not able to settle down. During this time it is best to wait out the meltdown. Do not address the behavior until there is calm and your child will be able to express what was happening. And know it may need to wait until the next day. As the parent, instead of swearing at them or threatening them with empty words, stop what you are doing and as calmly as you can remove yourself and your child from the situation. Being a parent of any special needs child takes an exceptional ability to be selfless and understanding. And yes, we are human and some days we will not have the best self control. Don't beat yourself up. Be kind to yourself and know that you can learn from each situation and move on.

Thankfully, there are people to help you within your community. Call your family service center and they can guide you. Ask your healthcare provider for direction on therapy and skills help. Be picky for yourself as well as your family. If the first person does not work out, keep looking until you find the right team. I was blessed when Kristi came into our lives. She has been with us for three years. I love that she has been here and walked through the good and the bad with us. She knows Parker and is able to call him on situations that may come up. She has also seen his growth and encourages him. The consistency is important for the child and the family. We had seen many therapists over a two year time period, and then we started seeing Joy. She is amazing with Parker as well as me and Parkers' dad. She has a laid back way of allowing Parker to be the driver yet she still has control. There is a soft spoken way about her that makes it easy for you to express and open up your thoughts. Parker can sometimes be abrasive in his tone. I am in awe of watching Joy as she interacts with him to bring him back to a non-frustrated point. Play and art therapy is a wonderful non-threatening way to help a child express themselves. When Parker was younger, I would give him a box, a button, ribbon, glue and paper to play with. This was relaxing for him. Now I am teaching him how to use paints. He has learned to interpret his feelings with color. In using the paints, he has learned to manage his anger and how to express it in a non- judgmental way. He has been drawing for years as well; he wants to be a designer when he grows up. He has several clothing designs that he has put together. This is how he was able to express himself to others for the longest time. When using art, there is no right or wrong, just freedom to be. Parker also took gymnastics. He was in a small group and it was non- competitive. He was there to learn and grow in his skills of interacting with other children as well as taking direction and constructive criticism.

Reading is a way he can calm himself. He is full of information. He knows much about things that you would never give the time to think about. Each night before bed, he will read for thirty minutes. He loves to read facts and informative book.

As Parker's mom, I have the responsibility to teach him different ways to express and cope. It would be an injustice to him if I did not teach him how to deal with daily life situations. At this moment in time, he may not understand why I have tough love and expectations of him. As he takes each step forward, he will start to see why things happen in his life and hopefully, he will have a better understanding.

Much of the work done with Aspergers children (and Aspergers adults) is to learn empathy and how to put someone else before themselves. Caring of others does not come naturally for them. They can see how others have done an injustice to them, and they can hold on to it forever, yet it is hard to see themselves and how they affect others with their own behaviors.

Parker has a friend whose Poppa died. Parker had said to me one day "Mom, I am sad for my friend, but I do not understand or know what to do.

I want to say something, yet I can't. Mom, is this empathy?" I wanted to cry to see his compassion for his friend; this is a big step for him to have a little understanding of what it is to care for someone like this.

He has also seen that his words can hurt people. Recently he was going through a hard situation. His behaviors had regressed, he had gotten frustrated, and in public he told me to 'shut up'. His day continued to worsen, he walked in the kitchen where I was, and he saw that I had been crying. He asked if it was because of how he had treated me. I was honest, and said "yes." In that moment he felt sorrow for his actions; this was a moment of growth for him.

It's getting easier for us in our home; we still have moments that I will have to ask our guest to leave. Family and friends have learned to accept Parker for who he is, and to take the time to go into his world.

There may be difficulties, but there are also many rewards. He still has times where he can be frustrated, but now we can get to a point where he can use his words. He is learning that sometimes he can settle his own self down by remembering to breathe as well as using his visual skills. Parker loves to ride rollercoasters; he will take himself to that place and it helps his anxiety.

In therapy, he has been working on writing down his feelings and thoughts when they come up. He is learning how to put his words into feelings, and then share those feelings. He may not always share them with the person that needs to know, but he will share with me or one of his team members. Sharing has been a *Big Victory* for Parker. Some things he chooses to keep between himself and his therapist. He has gotten brave over the past few months to express himself, and has been able to talk through and work on situations that have come up. This is a wonderful thing for him, and the people who are in his life. It's wonderful for me too! As Parker's mom, I will be an advocate for him when it is needed. It has been good for me not to be in the middle of situations that I do not fully understand.

I most often hear Parker's side, and with the Aspergers I have learned there can be drama. It's not to say that he is not sharing is the truth. He can get worked up sometimes. All right, often. One thing that Joy and I have noticed is you can ask Parker how it is going. If all is well in that moment, he will answer "fine." He may have had a total melt down an hour, a day or a week ago. But at that moment, he does not or is unable to recall those thoughts. He needs a cue to help him to remember situations. I'm not sure if this happens with others that have Aspergers, or if for some reason the anxiety has this effect on him.

When the parents are divorced, having open communication and understanding of their child's needs is helpful to all involved. If you are unable to talk with your former spouse, use a note book to say what needs to be said. Keeping the same routine at both homes so the child will have consistency is helpful to the child and the parents. Parker's dad and I are working more each day on how we can make transitions easy and comfortable for Parker. We are also teaching him that it's all right if he feels uncomfortable. This is a great chance for him to learn how to be open, as well as to know that differences can be a good thing and to at least try.

Parker was gone at his dad's over a school break. He had several moments that he thought he wanted to come home before his week was up. However, he was able to push past fears and tell himself that he can do it! He stayed and he felt so proud and victorious. The transition coming home can be hard for Parker. He has much to say. I was proud that he shared the good times and fun things that happened before he shared what upset him.

It had been a harder visit for Parker. His dad's schedule had a last minute change at his job, so Parker had to spend time at his grandma's. He loves his grandma, but all the change from one place to the next tested him and the skills he had learned. He shared that he had fun, but there were times that were difficult, so he went by himself to have a moment if he needed to cry.

Now he will need to decompress. This can be hard for both Parker as well as me. Parker can be mouthy and test the water. I wish that I could say that I always do a great job and never lose it, but I can't. I am human and I can take only so many attitudes before I'm done. I have learned many ways to help Parker decompress from situations that have come up for him, but there are those times where he does not stop and listen. He is always sorry after all is said and done, but while we're in the midst of whatever it is he needs to do or say, that time can be difficult. I want him to be able to express openly what is going on inside of him while making sure that he isn't out of control.

There are times that he cannot stop himself, and the anger he is feeling becomes rage. As he's gotten older, he is able to see what he is like after the fact when this happens. There have been a few times he has said to me that he is unable to stop himself. I have learned that time in his room alone is good for him in these moments. If he has extra energy, I will let him play a building game on the computer and I will not put a time limit on how long he can play. It has taken time to realize what is helpful, and what will cause more harm and upset. As we go through each stage of his life, we are both growing and moving forward.

There are some things about Parker that he may always have issues with. He does not understand jokes or sarcasms. When I speak to him, I will always need to say what I mean. His mind is literal, and that is how he processes. When you need him to do something, or you are giving him directions, be clear in what is meant. Parker has a hard time with fears. For years, it was hard for him to have the door closed. Even when he went to the bathroom, the door had to stay open even a crack.

At school, he was uncomfortable using the bathroom because of his fear of closed doors. He's scared of water. Not only is he afraid of drowning, but he has sensory issues to deal with. He cannot stand having water in his face.

This explains why bath time and head washing is a battle. We deal with food textures. He will only eat some foods. Too many textures in a dish can be hard for him; there are many textures at once. We did go to Occupational Therapist (OT) and he received help in some areas of food as well as showering. They taught Parker to wear goggles in the shower to help keep the water out of his face. He has sampled many foods to find the ones that he will eat. I have learned that he is a cruncher. In stressful moments, he will eat foods that he can crunch. He loves chips, and he will eat veggies that crunch as well. Although he does not care much for meat, he loves chicken and would eat it every day.

I have noticed as well that some fruits can and have change in his demeanor. Citrus fruits, as well as strawberries, can make his mood more intense. I allow him to eat them because he loves them; I just do it in moderation. He does not care much for dairy. He has never been a milk drinker. He will sometimes have cheese and ice cream occasionally. There are so many great products out there that taste good and are a good substantiation for dairy. He has wheat in moderations. He does not care for the texture of bread, but he loves bagels.

In the winter time he often does not put on his coat. The temperatures on a normal winter day do not affect him. He does get cold when it's below freezing. Likewise, in the summer the heat does not affect him. He will wear a hoodie, or a few shirts on a hot day, and still be comfortable.

Parker was not vaccinated, so there is no link to his Aspergers. We use medications to help with his tics and his anxiety. As he grows, he may learn coping skills, and his anxiety will not be as overwhelming for him. With the Tourettes, he may have tics for the rest of his life and will need the use of medication to help with the chemical imbalance. As his parent, I do not believe that using medication is a bad thing for him. He is regularly monitored by a doctor. Over time, I have learned that his doctor has his best interest foremost. We also use essential oils as well music and art to help calm him. The combination seems to work well for Parker. If you are anti-medication, please know that I am not judging your opinions on how you choose to treat your child. I see every situation as a unique and individual.

Parker does all right at school. He loves to learn and he understands most things quickly. Sometimes his brain can go faster than he can keep up with and he will get frustrated. Math is a particular source of frustration for him; reading and spelling come more naturally.

His hand writing can be a bit messy. He worked on in both in OT, as well as with Kristi during skills. We have all noticed that his brain can run faster than the thought he is having. As he is writing, he is unable to get his thoughts out fast enough, so his writing becomes "messy!" We do homework in 20 minute increments. This seems to work well for him, and he is productive. If the work is something that is harder and is causing him frustration, we do a little at a time so he can get the understanding of what he is doing without being over whelmed. We have a 504 plan for him that lists his needs. I will continue to seek out getting him an IEP, so he will be able to receive the help that he needs as he goes through school. It has been my understanding and experience that getting an IEP is a difficult task.

What was noticed during school is that he can be obsessed about staying on task, and sometimes he worries so much about staying right on task that he can obsess, then rush himself to make sure he is at the next point. Some of his teachers have been helpful. For the most part, they have taken the time to work with Parker. The lunchroom is overwhelming for him. It is a small room and full of noise. He often gets to eat lunch up stairs with a staff member. And on the days that he must stay, he eats quickly, and then goes to the library where there is less noise. He also has a free pass to go to the school's social worker as needed. The kids in school like him. He has a few friends that he would consider good friends. They are girls, and seem to be a year or so younger. He is often teased, mainly by the boys, for some of his choices. He is learning that it is all right to be different, and to be true to himself. He's not a sports kind of guy. He loves art and creating. It's important to teach your child that no matter what, they can be who they want to be, as long as it does not hurt anyone. I think academically Parker will do well. Sometimes he may need to be challenged, so he will not get bored. At this moment, he needs to be taught not to blame others and to be responsible for himself.

As the parent, this is a minute by minute in the world of an Aspergers and/or Tourettes child. Being open and flexible will make life easier for everyone. It's not a wise decision to need to go head-to-head and always have to be right with your child. Why does it matter if you are right? What is it teaching your child? As with all children and people, learn to pick your battles. If you say you're going to do something, follow through and have integrity, whether it is discipline or doing something fun. When you say something, be clear and mean it; do not be wishy washy. Consistency is the most important thing for a child with Aspergers. They need consistent dinner time, bed time, homework time as well as time with family and friends. Consistent time with their team members is important, as well as having down time to be alone in their own special place, doing what they enjoy. If the child lives with both parents, tag team with one another so one person is not doing all the giving, and both of you have time to refuel. If the parents are no longer together, try to work together for the needs of the child.

Share what works and what is important so the child will enjoy and feel safe at either home. If you are unable to discuss things about the child's needs, work through your therapist. And take the time to be a part of your child's therapy. If you are the non-custodial parent, and you do not wish to be a part of the meetings, please take a moment to call and ask for updates or input.

For those of you who are friends or family and do not live in our homes, and you're on the outside looking in, I say to you: have an open mind and do not be critical and opinionated. There are many good books and information out there that can give you a greater understanding.

If you have a friend or a family member that has a child with special needs, ask questions and offer to give them some of your time to watch their child. Aspergers is not contagious, so you will not get it! And Tourettes can only be offensive if you allow yourself to be offended. You must be willing to think and give out of your comfort zone, and to pay attention to the child.

If the music is blasting and you see that the child is holding their ears and seems antsy, the loud music might be a stimulation overload for them. At this time, it may be best to turn the music down. If they seem to be in their own world, you can try asking what they would like to do, or maybe they need time in their own space.

I have the most wonderful friends. My best friend Shari would often sneak over to my house and she would go down stairs and do my laundry.

I would come home from a long day at work and she had cleaned my home and put a fresh pot of coffee on. Before we knew about the Aspergers, she was concerned for Parker as well as my own well-being. She saw him lose control. She also sat and listened to him as he would pour his heart out over situations that were put into his life that he had no idea how to comprehend. Shari and her husband Mike opened up their family to us. Shari listened to me cry when I did not know what I was going to do. She never judged me. She sometimes came over with white chocolate and a bottle of my favorite wine and endless hours of sharing. Thank you, my beautiful friend; you will always be a jewel in my crown.

Parker and I have a friend named Tom. I have known Tom for almost twenty years. He has been in all my children's lives. He is wonderful with Parker. Tom will go into Parker's world, and take time to teach and listen.

When we get together, Tom usually has a question of interest for Parker that makes him think. I love that they're both a couple of kids and that Tom is not concerned what he looks like. He is there to give and have a good time. Parker painted Tom a picture of his version of "A Starry Night." The painting hangs proudly in Tom's house. When Parker loses it in front of Tom, Tom is good at helping to calm him. When he swears or yells, Tom redirects him or allows him to be. Never does he shame him, or make him feel less of a person.

I'm grateful for the people that are in our lives. They want to be here, and they are flexible with the needs of any situations that may come up.

My friend Chris is so good to see when I'm frazzled and need a moments break from all the whys and how comes that Parker asks. She steps in and takes over answering the questions.

One Halloween, Parker wanted to be a black cat. I was a mess from just moving out of our home, going to school and trying to find a job. The thought of running all over town looking for a cat costume was the last thing on my mind. Chris stepped in and helped with all the obstacles. As Parker got mad and hit me because the stores did not have what he wanted, Chris calmly talked to him. Without judgments or comments, she had compassion and understanding. At that time, we did not know about the Aspergers. We thought that it was situational. Chris is very kind, and teaches instead of demands and looses it. Parker loves his time at her home. We are lucky to have her in our lives. Thank you for being who you are, and all that you do!

My older kids are awesome! My daughter Lynley had a harder time because she lived in our home. Sometimes she was Parker's caregiver. Because of situations that came up, Lynley went to live with her older brother her senior year of high school. Parker's rage could be so bad that it was unsafe for others to be in our home. Now they have an exceptional relationship. Lynley is married, and a mom herself. Parker spends time at her home with her husband, Vince. Parker loves his nephew and is very gentle with him. He often shares with me that he can tell Lynley anything that is going on his heart.

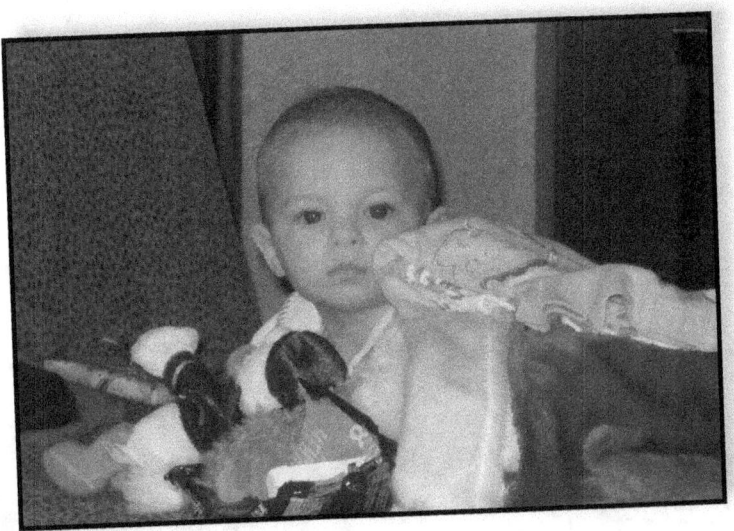

He loves spending time with his older brother, Sean, and his wife, Rachel. Parker thinks that they are cool and fun. They both have a passion for art and things that are a little non-conventional. Parker fits into their world. Parker loves art as well as being a little bit different. They will take him for the day, and do things that show him ways to 'think outside of the box.' This can be a hard task for Parker. It's funny to watch and listen to them having a conversation. Parker can have a *literal* thought or question as he's trying to "think outside the box."

Parker and his cousin Jesse are good friends. Jesse is a year and a half older and has helped teach Parker different life skills along the way. It's amazing to watch Jesse as he takes his time and goes step-by-step in showing Parker how to do something. He does not get upset and there never is a feeling of "what's wrong with you." I see the two of them growing up to be good, lifelong friends. Jesse has two sisters, Paulina and Ang (aka Sweetie). Parker gets along with them as well.

Parker has an Uncle and Aunt that have been very gracious to us. He allows us to rent his home, and has made it affordable for me to do so. This is important for Parker to have a place that feels like home to him, and that is stable. Parker loves to spend time with them as well. His Uncle takes the time to answer Parker's questions. Once Parker had a question about his family, so his uncle had us over to his home and got out the old photos and he told Parker stories about their family. Parker took in all that he said, and to this day remembers the details. One time, Parker's grandma and uncle were together with some cousins for a visit. Parker said he listened for hours about his family. He enjoys history of any kind. As he takes it in, he remembers what has been said, or when he reads, he remembers the facts that he read.

As Parker grows, we will encounter new situations and many questions. He already asks, "Why is it that I have hair growing on my legs and fingers, again?" "Will I need to start shaving soon?" The differences for us going through life changes are the obsessions, and there will be many detailed, never-ending questions. I try to answer to the point, with only the facts and not to use extra words. Too many words can make conversations confusing, so keep it simple. This is a phrase that we have posted in our home…

"Keep It Simple!!"

Parker is ten. He still likes to cuddle and he has items that comfort him. He may need these items for awhile yet. I think it is important for his growth to allow him to go through each stage, as well as to have all the needs met without making him feel shamed or embarrassed.

My son loves to talk and to ask questions. Most kids his age have many questions. Parker's questions can sometimes be odd, or a bit extreme.

There are no stupid questions. You may get tired of all that are continuously asked, and the non-stop talking. There is always an answer, even if it is, "I'm not sure!" And if you need a break, say so; they're not mind readers.

I look forward to the future to see how time changes our lives. I believe that if you seek help and share in the growth, you can learn to be more each day. You may always have a disability, but do not let it disable you. Live life one day, one minute at a time and learn something new each day!

Self-care is very important as a caregiver to a special needs child. As a single mom, I had to learn to allow others to help me. Parker is on a schedule and for the most part I keep him on it. I do this not only for him, but for me as well. I know by 8:15 I will have quiet time to myself. Some days I will sit in the silence. Sometimes I will call a friend or my sister. I had to learn that even though there may be dishes in the sink and clothes to be washed, they will wait because I need to stop and give myself time to relax and refuel.

I once said to someone, "I am Aspergers." However, I was incorrect. We have Aspergers and Tourettes in our home, but it does not define who I am as a person. I am compassionate, fun, loving and a bit sassy! I love to listen to music, write and paint. I love to laugh with my friends. I enjoy sitting in the quietness of my back yard with a cup of coffee on a starry night. Recently, I went back to school. It's hard work. I do it for me, and I am enjoying the growth. I love time with my kid and I adore my grandson. I love the way his face lights up when we spend time together. When I am with Parker, life is a bit rigid and predictable. When I am by myself or with friends, I am spontaneous and carefree.

Someday, I hope to find love that will not judge, and will want to 'Be' for no other reason than because. And in that there will be a freedom to give as well as to be given to.

As the caregivers, be kind to yourself. Find what will bring you peace and happiness. Never be ashamed or too proud to ask for help or to take help. This is not a sign of weakness; it's a sign of strength.

The Last Dance

Helping Others to Have Understanding

On the outside looking in
Confused with what you see?
Does it scare you this unknown?
Frighten of what may be?

Come on in and be a friend
Please don't be afraid of me
I am a person with a heart
A friend is all I want to be

I may need understanding
And time to re-think my thoughts
I can be over active, this I don't mean to be
Inside of me this is who I am
All I need is for you to try to understand
And to be a friend

E. Sheehan, 2008

The last thing I would like to share with you is that if you know a person with Aspergers, have understanding. Not only of whom the person is, but also asks what the person needs are and what they will be able to handle. Parker has been exposed to a number of things that cause him a *tremendous* amount of unnecessary anxiety. If you are unsure of what is right or wrong for the child, *ask the parent*. You may introduce the child to something that will harm them. O.C.D. is a big part of Asperger's, at least for Parker it is. If you allow a child to do something and they get fixated on it, life can be a living hell for everyone involved as you try to add a positive to replace the negative. There is a great deal that is involved when you are trying to redirect a situation. This is important to know, you can't just say to the child "get over it," or "you need to learn how to cope with the issue." To continue to put these issues in their world can cause damage. With anxiety there is a higher level of OCD, there is no stopping the child if they get stuck. There can be nightmares, sleep walking, unable to concentrate at school, they will talk about it non-stop. As the parent you have to ride it out and pray that it will end soon. There is no reason for a child to struggle. Please do not guess if it will be all right or not. Ask questions.

If you are parents that live in different homes, communication is a must.

As the non-custodial parent, ask questions of the parent that lives daily with all the issues that come up. For the child, have some humility to ask the questions and to have follow through. Letting your child know the events ahead of time will save them a great deal of stress from the unknown. They are creatures of "I need to know." We have had sleepless nights over the fears of what may or may not be. A phone call the day before can help!

Be careful of what you share with your child. They are not little adults or your best friend. The less drama that is put into their world is going to help them to stay calm. Their minds are full enough of their own world. They do not need yours as well. They do not always have understanding of the actions that they may see, so it is important to pay attention to your own actions. They also have greater senses. They can hear a whisper from the next room. Use wisdom in your decisions.

I love my son, and I am proud of his growth. It's amazing to watch him go from no steps, to baby steps and now he's taking *GIANT* steps to overcome his fears. This takes time and patience. Most of all, it takes a team that works well together and will stay with the family, even when it gets hard. We have been blessed with this team. We have the *Best* team one could ask for.

Last words from Parker,

Having Aspergers does not make us weirdoes. We are people who love to have fun, to learn, to share and to laugh. We are artistic, intelligent people. We can be talkers, and okay we just love to talk about ourselves, so we may need a reminder that we are not the only one in the room. I need for others to listen and to understand who I am.

We are Human, and we can make mistakes, and in this, we can learn.
Thank you for dancing with us!

My favorite quote...

"Everything precious including our
dignity can be taken from us but the
one thing that cannot be taken is our
power to choose what attitude we will take
toward the events that have happened "

Viktor Frankl

References

Skills Therapist: Kristi Brown, LMFT. Generation, 2649 Park Avenue South Minneapolis, MN 55407

Play Therapist: Joy Petermann, MSW, LICSW. 5775 Wayzata Blvd. Suite 700 St. Louis Park, MN 55416

Helpful, fun reading:

"All cats have aspergers syndrome" Author, Kathy Hoopmann

Fumia, M. Safe Passages, A quote by Viktor Frankl

www.ingramcontent.com/pod-product-compliance
Lightning Source LLC
Chambersburg PA
CBHW052016280526

45793CB00005B/998